Low Fat™

GREAT-TASTING

KIDS' SNACKS

Healthy & Delicious Recipes

PUBLICATIONS INTERNATIONAL, LTD.

Recipe Development: Karen Levin, Food Consultant; Sue Spitler, Food Consultant, Incredible Edibles, Ltd.
Nutritional Analysis: Linda R. Yoakam, M.S., R.D.

Photography: Sacco Productions Limited, Chicago
Photographers: Tom O'Connell, Rick Tragesser
Photo Stylist: Melissa J. Frisco
Production: Paula M. Walters
Food Stylists: Mary Ann Melone, Carol Parik, Teri Rys-Maki
Assistant Food Stylist: Kim Hartman

Pictured on the front cover *(clockwise from top left):* Cinnamon Trail Mix *(page 38),* Gingerbread Squares *(page 32)* and Perfect Pita Pizzas *(page 74).*
Pictured on the inside front cover: Super Nachos *(page 84).*
Pictured on the inside back cover: Bamboozlers *(page 62).*
Pictured on the back cover *(counterclockwise from top right):* Yuletide Twisters *(page 22),* Fruit and Oat Squares *(page 42),* Banana Freezer Pops *(page 80)* and Taco Popcorn Olé *(page 58).*

ISBN: 0-7853-1556-X

Manufactured in U.S.A.

8 7 6 5 4 3 2 1

Microwave Cooking: Microwave ovens vary in wattage. The microwave cooking times given in this publication are approximate. Use the cooking times as guidelines and check for doneness before adding more time. Consult manufacturer's instructions for suitable microwave-safe cooking dishes.

CONTENTS

Lessons in Smart Eating

Today, people everywhere are more aware than ever before about the importance of maintaining a healthful lifestyle. In addition to proper exercise, this includes eating foods that are lower in fat, sodium and cholesterol. The goal of this book is to provide today's cook with easy-to-prepare recipes that taste great, yet easily fit into your dietary goals. Eating well is a matter of making smarter choices about the foods you eat. Preparing these recipes is your first step toward making smart choices a delicious reality.

A Balanced Diet

The U.S. Department of Agriculture and the Department of Health and Human Services have developed a Food Guide Pyramid to illustrate how easy it is to eat a healthier diet. It is not a rigid prescription, but rather a general guide that lets you choose a healthful diet that's right for you. It calls for eating a wide variety of foods to get the nutrients you need and, at the same time, the right amount of calories to maintain a healthy weight.

Food Guide Pyramid
A Guide to Daily Food Choices

Fats, Oils, & Sweets
Use Sparingly
(Also found in other
groups; see text.)

KEY
•Fat (naturally occurring ▾Sugar
and added) (added)
These symbols show fats, oils, and
added sugars in foods.

Milk, Yogurt,
& Cheese
Group
2–3 Servings

Meat, Poultry, Fish,
Dry Beans, Eggs,
& Nuts Group
2–3 Servings

Vegetable Group
3–5 Servings

Fruit Group
2–4 Servings

Bread, Cereal,
Rice, & Pasta
Group
6–11
Servings

The number of servings, and consequently, the number of calories a person can eat each day, is determined by a number of factors, including age, weight, height and activity level. Suggested calorie levels for children aged 1-10 years are as follows: 1 to 3 years - 1300 calories; 4 to 6 years - 1800 calories; 7 to 10 years - 2000 calories. Although the number of food group servings for the different age groups remains the same, the serving size for each age group varies.

Personalized Food Group Serving Sizes for Different Age Groups			
	1–3 years of age	4–6 years of age	7–10 years of age
Bread Group Serving Size	½ slice	1 slice	1–2 slices
Vegetable Group Serving Size	2–4 Tbsp.	¼ –½ cup	½–¾ cup
Fruit Group Serving Size	2–4 Tbsp. or ½ cup juice	¼ –½ cup or ½ cup juice	½–¾ cup or ½ cup juice
Milk Group Serving Size	½ – ¾ cup	¾ cup	¾–1 cup
Meat Group Serving Size	1–2 ounces	1–2 ounces	2–3 ounces

Lower Fat for Healthier Living

It is widely known that most Americans' diets are too high in fat. A low fat diet reduces your risk of getting certain diseases and helps you maintain a healthy weight. Studies have shown that eating more than the recommended amount of fat (especially saturated fat) is associated with increased blood cholesterol levels in some adults. A high blood cholesterol level is associated with increased risk for heart disease. A high fat diet may also increase your chances for obesity and some types of cancer.

Nutrition experts recommend diets that contain 30% or less of total daily calories from fat. The "30% calories from fat" goal applies to a total diet over time, not to a single food, serving of a recipe or meal. To find the approximate percentage of calories from fat use this easy 3-step process:

1 Multiply the grams of fat per serving by 9 (there are 9 calories in each gram of fat), to give you the number of calories from fat per serving.

2 Divide by the total number of calories per serving.

3 Multiply by 100%.

For example, imagine a 200 calorie sandwich that has 10 grams of fat.
To find the percentage of calories from fat, first multiply the grams of fat by 9:
$$10 \times 9 = 90$$

Then, divide by the total number of calories in a serving:
$$90 \div 200 = .45$$

Multiply by 100% to get the percentage of calories from fat:
$$.45 \times 100\% = 45\%$$

You may find doing all this math tiresome, so an easier way to keep track of the fat in your diet is to calculate the total *grams* of fat appropriate to your caloric intake, then keep a running count of fat grams over the course of a day. The Nutrition Reference Chart on page 92 lists recommended daily fat intakes based on calorie level.

Defining "Fat Free"

It is important to take the time to read food labels carefully. For example, you'll find many food products on the grocery store shelves making claims such as "97% fat free." This does not necessarily mean that 97% of the *calories* are free from fat (or that only 3 percent of calories come from fat). Often these numbers are calculated by weight. This means that out of 100 grams of this food, 3 grams are fat. Depending on what else is in the food, the percentage of calories from fat can be quite high. You may find that the percent of calories *from fat* can be as high as 50%.

Daily Values

Fat has become the focus of many diets and eating plans. This is because most Americans' diets are too high in fat. However, there are other important nutrients to be aware of, including saturated fat, sodium, cholesterol, protein, carbohydrates and several vitamins and minerals. Daily values for these nutrients have been established by the government and reflect current nutritional recommendations for a 2,000 calorie reference diet. They are appropriate for most adults and children (age 4 or older) and provide excellent guidelines for an overall healthy diet. The chart on page 92 gives the daily values for 11 different items.

Nutritional Analysis

Every recipe is followed by a nutritional analysis block that lists certain nutrient values for a single serving.

■ The analysis of each recipe includes all the ingredients that are listed in that recipe, except ingredients labeled as "optional" or "for garnish." Nutritional analysis is provided for the primary recipe only—not for the recipe variations.

■ If a range is offered for an ingredient ("¼ to ⅛ teaspoon" for example), the first amount given was used to calculate the nutrition information.

■ If an ingredient is presented with an option ("whole wheat or white pita bread rounds", for example), the first item listed was used to calculate the nutritional information.

■ Foods shown in photographs on the same serving plate and offered as "serve with" suggestions at the end of a recipe are not included in the recipe analysis unless they are listed in the ingredient list.

■ Ingredient substitutions may be made in many of the recipes included in this publication. For example, whole milk, 2% low fat milk and skim milk can often be used interchangeably. Likewise, cream cheese may be used instead of nonfat cream cheese or Neufchâtel cheese, and regular Cheddar cheese can be used instead of reduced fat or nonfat Cheddar cheese.

The nutrition information that appears with each recipe was calculated by an independent nutrition consulting firm. Every effort has been made to check the accuracy of these numbers. However, because numerous variables account for a wide range of values in certain foods, all analyses that appear in this book should be considered approximate.

The recipes in this publication are not intended as a medically therapeutic program, nor as a substitute for medically approved diet plans for people on fat, cholesterol or sodium restricted diets. You should consult your child's physician before beginning any diet plan. The recipes offered here can be a part of a healthy lifestyle that meets recognized dietary guidelines. A healthy lifestyle includes not only eating a balanced diet, but engaging in proper exercise as well.

All the ingredients called for in these recipes are generally available in large supermarkets, so there is no need to go to specialty or health food stores. You'll also see an ever-increasing amount of reduced fat and nonfat products available in local markets. Take advantage of these items to reduce your daily fat intake even more.

With today's increasing focus on nutrition, it's only natural that this awareness should encompass the snacks we offer our children. However, finding nutritious snacks that actually appeal to youngsters can be frustrating. This fabulous collection of kid-pleasing recipes solves this dilemma with dozens of irresistible yet nutritious snacks sure to satisfy even the most finicky eaters.

Low Fat Great-Tasting Kids' Snacks offers fun recipes specially created for kids of all ages. So, whether you're trying to feed a classroom full of preschoolers or satisfy the seemingly endless hunger pangs of a preteen, you're sure to find delicious ideas here. Your most difficult task will be deciding which one of these dazzling treats to make first!

For the family on the go, most of these tempting snacks call for only a few ingredients and can be made in just a matter of minutes. Many of these recipes are also simple enough for a child to supply that extra set of hands always appreciated in the kitchen. But best of all, these marvelous snacks not only taste good, they're actually good for you, too. But, let's keep that a secret!

For the younger set, the "Preschool Nibbles" chapter features whimsical snacks sure to bring a smile to a child's face. Trying to satisfy a sweet tooth? Fanciful Tooty Fruitys or dazzling Ice Cream Cone Cakes is bound to win raves. And, after sampling the Purple Cow Jumped over the Moon frothy milk shake, you too will want to join in on the fun. No matter what your choice, each fun-to-eat delight is sure to make snack time the favorite time of day!

Need some creative ways to erase the lunch box blues? Page through "Lunch Box Treats" for a playful assortment of totable snacks. Many can even be prepared ahead and thrown into a lunch box at the last minute to make hectic mornings less frantic. For added convenience, some treats can be stored in the freezer. Just pop them frozen into lunch boxes in the morning and by noon they're thawed and ready to eat. What child doesn't like s'mores? Nonmessy, chocolatey Quick S'Mores are sure to be the envy of the cafeteria. Who knows? After tasting our crunchy Fruit and Oat Squares, Crispy Savory Pita Chips and colorful Cinnamon Trail Mix, you may add one of these tasty gems to your own lunch box!

Room moms listen up! There are creative ideas designed just for you in the "School Party Snacks" chapter. For extra fun, most of these tantalizing tidbits can be decorated to fit the holiday at hand. Need a hauntingly delectable Halloween idea? Try refreshing Trick or Treat Ice Cream Sandwiches and start the party off right. For the festive holidays, Sweet Holidays Pizza is sure to be a winner. Or, surprise your Valentine's Day sweetie with heart-shaped Soft Pretzels. This fun-to-make savory bread will demand a repeat performance throughout the year!

Turn to the "After School Munchies" chapter for a bounty of snacks sure to fill up that forever-hungry late afternoon crowd. Many of these recipes can be prepared ahead or assembled in just minutes to satisfy ravenous kids right away. Keep an assortment of cut-up fresh vegetables in the refrigerator so the kids can transform pita bread halves into colorful pizzas in a flash. Let them whip up Super Nachos in less than 5 minutes with the help of the microwave oven. Or, team up ripe bananas with tangy orange juice for fun frozen ice pop treats. It's a winning combination!

After sampling these scrumptious snacks, you'll be convinced that good taste and nutrition can go hand in hand. Start subscribing today to a healthier way of providing between meal foods for your children. Enjoy!

PRESCHOOL NIBBLES

SEÑOR NACHO DIP

All the flavors of Mexico are captured in this cheesy, low fat dip. When served with baked tortilla chips, only 18% of the calories come from fat.

4 ounces nonfat cream cheese
½ cup (2 ounces) reduced fat Cheddar cheese
¼ cup mild or medium chunky salsa
2 teaspoons 2% low fat milk
4 ounces baked tortilla chips or assorted fresh vegetable dippers

1 Combine cream cheese and Cheddar cheese in small saucepan; stir over low heat until melted. Stir in salsa and milk; heat thoroughly, stirring occasionally.

2 Transfer dip to small serving bowl. Serve with tortilla chips. Garnish with hot pepper and cilantro, if desired.

Makes 4 servings

Olé Dip: Substitute reduced fat Monterey Jack cheese or taco cheese for Cheddar cheese.

Spicy Mustard Dip: Omit tortilla chips. Substitute 2 teaspoons spicy brown or honey mustard for salsa. Serve with fresh vegetable dippers or pretzels.

Nutrients per Serving:

Calories	181
(18% of calories from fat)	
Total Fat	4 g
Saturated Fat	1 g
Cholesterol	11 mg
Sodium	629 mg
Carbohydrate	25 g
Dietary Fiber	2 g
Protein	11 g
Calcium	309 mg
Iron	<1 mg
Vitamin A	143 RE
Vitamin C	5 mg

DIETARY EXCHANGES:
1½ Starch/Bread, 1 Lean Meat

PURPLE COW JUMPED OVER THE MOON

*Milk shakes are all-time
favorites with kids. Any one
of these fruity low fat shakes
is sure to win raves.*

3 cups vanilla nonfat frozen yogurt
1 cup 2% low fat milk
½ cup thawed frozen grape juice concentrate (undiluted)
1½ teaspoons lemon juice

1 Place yogurt, milk, grape juice concentrate and lemon juice in food processor or blender container; process until smooth. Serve immediately.

Makes 8 (½-cup) servings

Razzmatazz Shake: Place 1 quart vanilla nonfat frozen yogurt, 1 cup vanilla nonfat yogurt and ¼ cup chocolate nonfat syrup in food processor or blender container; process until smooth. Pour ½ of mixture evenly into 12 glasses; top with ½ of 12-ounce can root beer. Fill glasses equally with remaining yogurt mixture; top with remaining root beer.

Makes 12 (⅔-cup) servings

Sunshine Shake: Place 1 quart vanilla nonfat frozen yogurt, 1⅓ cups orange juice, 1 cup fresh or thawed frozen raspberries and 1 teaspoon sugar in food processor or blender container; process until smooth. Pour into 10 glasses; sprinkle with ground nutmeg.

Makes 10 (½-cup) servings

Nutrients per Serving:

Calories	123
(5% of calories from fat)	
Total Fat	<1 g
Saturated Fat	<1 g
Cholesterol	2 mg
Sodium	58 mg
Carbohydrate	26 g
Dietary Fiber	<1 g
Protein	3 g
Calcium	40 mg
Iron	<1 mg
Vitamin A	19 RE
Vitamin C	13 mg

DIETARY EXCHANGES:
1 Starch/Bread, ½ Fruit

FRUIT FREEZIES

*Try any of these favorite
fruit combinations or create
your own!*

Nutrients per Serving:

(2 cubes)

Calories	19
(1% of calories from fat)	
Total Fat	<1 g
Saturated Fat	<1 g
Cholesterol	0 mg
Sodium	2 mg
Carbohydrate	5 g
Dietary Fiber	<1 g
Protein	<1 g
Calcium	1 mg
Iron	<1 mg
Vitamin A	19 RE
Vitamin C	2 mg

DIETARY EXCHANGES:
½ Fruit

1½ cups (12 ounces) canned or thawed frozen peach slices, drained
¾ cup peach nectar
1 tablespoon sugar
¼ to ½ teaspoon coconut extract (optional)

1 Place peaches, nectar, sugar and extract in food processor or blender container; process until smooth.

2 Spoon 2 tablespoons fruit mixture into each section of ice cube trays.*

3 Freeze until almost firm. Insert frill pick into each cube; freeze until firm.

Makes 12 servings

*Or, pour ⅓ cup fruit mixture into each of 8 plastic pop molds or small paper or plastic cups. Freeze until almost firm. Insert wooden stick into each mold; freeze until firm.

Makes 8 servings

Apricot Freezies: Substitute canned apricot halves for peach slices and apricot nectar for peach nectar.

Mango Freezies: Omit coconut extract. Substitute chopped fresh mango for canned peach slices and mango nectar for peach nectar.

Pear Freezies: Substitute canned pear slices for peach slices, pear nectar for peach nectar and almond extract for coconut extract.

Pineapple Freezies: Substitute crushed pineapple for peach slices and unsweetened pineapple juice for peach nectar.

BERRY GOOD DIP

8 ounces fresh or thawed frozen strawberries
4 ounces nonfat cream cheese, softened
¼ cup reduced fat sour cream
1 tablespoon sugar

1 Place strawberries in food processor or blender container; process until smooth.

2 Beat cream cheese in small bowl until smooth. Stir in sour cream, strawberry purée and sugar; cover. Refrigerate until ready to serve.

3 Spoon dip into small serving bowl. Garnish with orange peel, if desired. Serve with assorted fresh fruit dippers or angel food cake cubes.   *Makes 6 (¼-cup) servings*

Raspberry Valentine Dip: Substitute 12 ounces raspberries for 8 ounces strawberries. Purée raspberries in food processor as directed; strain to remove seeds. Continue as directed.

Minted Valentine Dip: Prepare Berry Good Dip or Raspberry Valentine Dip as directed. Stir in ½ teaspoon dried mint leaves; cover. Refrigerate at least 2 hours for flavors to blend.

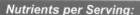

Nutrients per Serving:

Calories	47
(16% of calories from fat)	
Total Fat	1 g
Saturated Fat	<1 g
Cholesterol	7 mg
Sodium	120 mg
Carbohydrate	6 g
Dietary Fiber	1 g
Protein	3 g
Calcium	85 mg
Iron	<1 mg
Vitamin A	92 RE
Vitamin C	21 mg

DIETARY EXCHANGES:
½ Lean Meat, ½ Fruit

Cook's Tip

For a super quick fruit spread for toasted mini English muffins or bagels, beat 1 package (8 ounces) softened nonfat cream cheese in small bowl until fluffy. Stir in 3 to 4 tablespoons strawberry spreadable fruit. Season to taste with 1 to 2 teaspoons sugar, if desired. Makes 6 servings.

ICE CREAM CONE CAKES

Surprisingly low in calories and fat, these spectacular treats are sure to bring a smile to any child's face. For extra delight, decorate with candies and colored cake decorating gels to suit the holiday season!

1 package (18.25 ounces) devil's food cake mix plus ingredients to prepare mix
⅓ cup sour cream
1 package (2⅝ ounces) flat-bottomed ice cream cones (about 18 cones)
1¼ cups nonfat frozen yogurt (any flavor)
    Cake decorations or chocolate sprinkles

1 Preheat oven to 350°F. Grease and flour 8- or 9-inch round cake pan; set aside.

2 Prepare cake mix according to package directions, substituting sour cream for ⅓ cup of water and decreasing oil to ¼ cup.

3 Spoon ½ of the batter (about 2⅓ cups) evenly into ice cream cones, using about 2 tablespoons batter for each. Pour remaining batter into prepared cake pan.

4 Stand cones on cookie sheet. Bake cones and cake layer until wooden pick inserted into center of cake comes out clean, about 20 minutes for cones and about 35 minutes for cake layer. Cool on wire racks, removing cake from pan after 10 minutes. Reserve or freeze cake layer for another use.

5 Top each filled cone with ¼ cup scoop of frozen yogurt just before serving. Sprinkle with decorations as desired. Serve immediately.   *Makes 18 servings*

Holiday Cone Cakes: Prepare cake batter as directed. Spoon about 3 tablespoons cake batter into each of 12 flat-bottomed ice cream cones. Bake as directed; cool completely. Spread with reduced fat frosting. Decorate with colored cake decorating gels and candies to make Jack-O'-Lantern faces, Valentine hearts or Christmas wreaths.   *Makes 12 servings*

Ice Cream Cake Cups: Prepare cake batter as directed. Spoon about 3 tablespoons cake batter into each of 12 (4-ounce) custard cups. Bake as directed for Ice Cream Cone Cakes; cool completely. Top each serving with ¼ cup scoop of desired flavor reduced fat frozen yogurt and caramel or fudge nonfat topping.   *Makes 12 servings*

Ice Cream Cupcakes: Spoon all of batter into paper-lined muffin cups according to package directions for cupcakes; cool completely. Spread with desired flavor reduced fat frosting. Decorate as desired or top with a small scoop of any flavor nonfat frozen yogurt.   *Makes about 2½ dozen*

Nutrients per Serving:

Calories	95
(22% of calories from fat)	
Total Fat	2 g
Saturated Fat	1 g
Cholesterol	2 mg
Sodium	129 mg
Carbohydrate	17 g
Dietary Fiber	<1 g
Protein	2 g
Calcium	44 mg
Iron	<1 mg
Vitamin A	10 RE
Vitamin C	<1 mg

DIETARY EXCHANGES:
1 Starch/Bread, ½ Fat

YULETIDE TWISTERS

Pretzels are a great low fat snack. Dress them up with a creamy, sweet coating and colorful sprinkles and they're sure to be a hit!

1 (6-ounce) package premier white baking bars
4 teaspoons skim milk
4 teaspoons light corn syrup
8 ounces reduced salt pretzel twists (about 80)
   Cookie decorations, colored sugar or chocolate sprinkles

1 Cover baking sheet with waxed paper; set aside.

2 Melt baking bars in small saucepan over low heat, stirring constantly. Stir in skim milk and corn syrup. Do not remove saucepan from heat.

3 Holding pretzel with fork, dip 1 side of each pretzel into melted mixture to coat. Place, coated side up, on prepared baking sheet; immediately sprinkle with desired decorations. Refrigerate until firm, 15 to 20 minutes.   *Makes 10 servings*

Chocolate Twisters: Substitute 1 (6-ounce) package semisweet chocolate chips for premier white baking bars.

Caramel Dippity Do's: Heat 1 cup nonfat caramel sauce and ⅓ cup finely chopped pecans in small saucepan until warm. Pour into small serving bowl. Serve with pretzels for dipping.   *Makes 8 servings (about 2 tablespoons each)*

Chocolate Dippity Do's: Heat 1 cup nonfat hot fudge sauce and ⅓ cup finely chopped pecans or walnuts in small saucepan until warm. Pour into small serving bowl. Serve with pretzels for dipping.   *Makes 8 servings (about 2 tablespoons each)*

Nutrients per Serving:

Calories	196
(32% of calories from fat)	
Total Fat	7 g
Saturated Fat	4 g
Cholesterol	4 mg
Sodium	386 mg
Carbohydrate	30 g
Dietary Fiber	0 g
Protein	3 g
Calcium	12 mg
Iron	1 mg
Vitamin A	2 RE
Vitamin C	<1 mg

DIETARY EXCHANGES:
2½ Starch/Bread, 1½ Fat

TOOTY FRUITYS

Fill the flaky dough with your favorite cut-up fresh fruits—apples, apricots, peaches, plums, pears or pineapple.

1 package (10 ounces) extra-light flaky biscuits
10 (1½-inch) fruit pieces
1 egg white
1 teaspoon water
  Powdered sugar (optional)

1 Preheat oven to 425°F. Spray baking sheet with nonstick cooking spray; set aside.

2 Separate biscuits. Place on lightly floured surface. Roll with lightly floured rolling pin or flatten dough with fingers to form 3½-inch circles. Place 1 fruit piece in center of each circle. Bring 3 edges of dough up over fruit; pinch edges together to seal. Place on prepared baking sheet.

3 Beat egg white with water in small bowl; brush over dough.

4 Bake until golden brown, 10 to 15 minutes. Remove to wire rack to cool. Serve warm or at room temperature. Sprinkle with powdered sugar just before serving.

Makes 10 servings

Sweet Tooty Fruitys: Prepare dough circles as directed. Gently press both sides of dough circles into granulated or cinnamon-sugar to coat completely. Top with fruit and continue as directed, except do not brush with egg white mixture or sprinkle with powdered sugar.

Cheesy Tooty Fruitys: Prepare dough circles as directed. Top each circle with ½ teaspoon softened reduced fat cream cheese in addition to the fruit. Continue as directed.

Roly Polys: Prepare dough circles as directed. Place fruit piece on 1 side of each circle. Fold over 2 edges of dough to cover fruit. Roll up dough, jelly-roll fashion, to form "log" shape. Brush with egg white mixture or roll in granulated or cinnamon-sugar. Place, seam side down, on prepared baking sheet. Bake as directed.

Nutrients per Serving:

Calories	93
(24% of calories from fat)	
Total Fat	3 g
Saturated Fat	<1 g
Cholesterol	0 mg
Sodium	230 mg
Carbohydrate	16 g
Dietary Fiber	1 g
Protein	2 g
Calcium	9 mg
Iron	1 mg
Vitamin A	14 RE
Vitamin C	3 mg

DIETARY EXCHANGES:
½ Starch/Bread, ½ Fruit,
½ Fat

SWEET AS ANGELS' KISSES

Decorate with colored sugars to match the season. Or, for a more festive look, sprinkle with crushed peppermint candies before baking.

❖

4 egg whites, at room temperature
¼ teaspoon cream of tartar
⅛ teaspoon salt
1 cup granulated sugar
¼ teaspoon peppermint or mint extract or desired fruit-flavored flavoring
Few drops red or green food color
Cookie decorations or colored sugar

1 Preheat oven to 250°F. Cover baking sheets with parchment paper or aluminum foil; set aside.

2 Beat egg whites in large bowl with electric mixer until foamy. Add cream of tartar and salt; beat until soft peaks form. Gradually add sugar, beating until stiff peaks form. Beat in extract and food color.

3 Drop rounded tablespoonfuls of egg white mixture onto prepared baking sheets; sprinkle with cookie decorations.

4 Bake until cookies are firm to the touch and just beginning to brown around the edges, 35 to 45 minutes. Remove to wire rack to cool completely.

Makes 20 servings

Cocoa Kisses: Omit extract, food color and decorations. Beat egg white mixture as directed until stiff peaks form; fold in ⅓ cup unsweetened cocoa powder. Drop rounded tablespoonfuls of egg white mixture onto prepared baking sheets as directed; sprinkle lightly with chocolate sprinkles or finely chopped nuts. Continue as directed.

Coconut Clouds: Omit food color. Substitute coconut extract for peppermint extract and flaked coconut for decorations.

Banana Confetti Bites: Substitute banana extract for peppermint extract and yellow food color for red or green food color.

Pineapple Puffs: Substitute pineapple extract for peppermint extract, yellow food color for red or green food color, and flaked coconut or finely chopped pecans for decorations.

Nutrients per Serving:

(3 cookies)

Calories	42
(0% of calories from fat)	
Total Fat	0 g
Saturated Fat	0 g
Cholesterol	0 mg
Sodium	25 mg
Carbohydrate	10 g
Dietary Fiber	0 g
Protein	1 g
Calcium	1 mg
Iron	<1 mg
Vitamin A	0 RE
Vitamin C	0 mg

DIETARY EXCHANGES:
Free Food

SWEET TREAT TORTILLAS

In just minutes, these soft breadlike tortillas are transformed into creamy, sweet pinwheels the entire class is sure to enjoy.

4 (7- to 8-inch) flour tortillas
4 ounces Neufchâtel cheese, softened
¼ cup strawberry or other flavor spreadable fruit or preserves
1 medium banana, peeled and chopped

1 Spread each tortilla with 1 ounce Neufchâtel cheese and 1 tablespoon spreadable fruit; top with ¼ of the banana.

2 Roll up tortillas; cut crosswise into thirds.   *Makes 6 servings*

More Sweet Treats: Substitute your favorite chopped fruit for banana.

Cinnamon-Spice Treats: Omit spreadable fruit and banana. Mix small amounts of sugar, ground cinnamon and nutmeg into Neufchâtel cheese; spread evenly onto tortillas. Sprinkle lightly with desired amount of chopped pecans or walnuts. Top with chopped fruit, if desired; roll up. Cut crosswise into thirds.

Nutrients per Serving:

(2 pieces)

Calories	184
(32% of calories from fat)	
Total Fat	7 g
Saturated Fat	3 g
Cholesterol	17 mg
Sodium	191 mg
Carbohydrate	28 g
Dietary Fiber	1 g
Protein	4 g
Calcium	47 mg
Iron	1 mg
Vitamin A	42 RE
Vitamin C	2 mg

DIETARY EXCHANGES:
1 Starch/Bread, 1 Fruit,
1 Fat

LUNCH BOX TREATS

QUICK S'MORES

An easy snack that kids will want to prepare themselves. Better prepare an extra for that envious schoolmate!

1 whole graham cracker
1 large marshmallow
1 teaspoon hot fudge sauce

1 Break graham cracker in half crosswise. Place ½ of cracker on small paper plate or microwavable plate; top with marshmallow.

2 Spread remaining ½ of cracker with fudge sauce.

3 Place cracker with marshmallow in microwave. Microwave at HIGH 12 to 14 seconds or until marshmallow puffs up. Immediately place remaining cracker, fudge side down, over marshmallow. Press crackers gently to even out marshmallow layer. Cool completely.

Makes 1 serving

Nutrients per Serving:

Calories	69
(19% of calories from fat)	
Total Fat	2 g
Saturated Fat	1 g
Cholesterol	0 mg
Sodium	49 mg
Carbohydrate	13 g
Dietary Fiber	0 g
Protein	1 g
Calcium	11 mg
Iron	<1 mg
Vitamin A	3 RE
Vitamin C	0 mg

DIETARY EXCHANGES:
1 Starch/Bread

Cook's Tip

S'mores can be made the night before and wrapped in plastic wrap or sealed in a small plastic food storage bag. Store at room temperature until ready to pack in your child's lunch box the next morning.

GINGERBREAD SQUARES

Children will love this moist, spicy treat. Get the entire family involved by decorating the squares together with frostings and candies.

3 tablespoons margarine, softened
2 tablespoons light brown sugar
¼ cup molasses
1 egg white
1¼ cups all-purpose flour
½ teaspoon ground ginger
½ teaspoon ground cinnamon
½ teaspoon baking soda
¼ teaspoon salt
1 cup sweetened applesauce
Tube frostings, colored sugars, red hot cinnamon candies or other small candies (optional)

1 Preheat oven to 350°F. Spray 8-inch square baking pan with nonstick cooking spray; set aside.

2 Beat margarine and brown sugar with wooden spoon in medium bowl until well blended. Beat in molasses and egg white.

3 Combine dry ingredients in small bowl; mix well. Add to margarine mixture alternately with applesauce, mixing well after each addition. Pour batter into prepared pan.

4 Bake 25 to 30 minutes or until wooden pick inserted in center comes out clean. Cool completely on wire rack. Cut into squares. Frost and decorate, if desired.

Makes 9 servings

Nutrients per Serving:	
Calories	142
(25% of calories from fat)	
Total Fat	4 g
Saturated Fat	1 g
Cholesterol	0 mg
Sodium	190 mg
Carbohydrate	25 g
Dietary Fiber	1 g
Protein	3 g
Calcium	72 mg
Iron	2 mg
Vitamin A	47 RE
Vitamin C	<1 mg

DIETARY EXCHANGES:
1½ Starch/Bread, ½ Fat

SAVORY PITA CHIPS

More flavorful and healthful than most store-bought chips, these pita chips are sure to be a lunch box favorite.

2 whole wheat or white pita bread rounds
   Olive oil flavored nonstick cooking spray
3 tablespoons grated Parmesan cheese
1 teaspoon dried basil leaves, crushed
¼ teaspoon garlic powder

1 Preheat oven to 350°F. Cover baking sheet with aluminum foil; set aside.

2 Using small scissors, carefully split each pita bread round around edges; separate to form 2 rounds. Cut each round into 6 wedges.

3 Place wedges, rough side down, on prepared baking sheet; coat lightly with cooking spray. Turn wedges over; spray again.

4 Combine Parmesan cheese, basil and garlic powder in small bowl; sprinkle evenly over pita wedges.

5 Bake 12 to 14 minutes or until golden brown. Cool completely.

Makes 4 servings

Cinnamon Crisps: Substitute butter flavored cooking spray for olive oil flavored cooking spray, and 1 tablespoon sugar mixed with ¼ teaspoon ground cinnamon for Parmesan cheese, basil and garlic powder.

Nutrients per Serving:

Calories	108
(18% of calories from fat)	
Total Fat	2 g
Saturated Fat	1 g
Cholesterol	4 mg
Sodium	257 mg
Carbohydrate	18 g
Dietary Fiber	0 g
Protein	5 g
Calcium	77 mg
Iron	<1 mg
Vitamin A	13 RE
Vitamin C	<1 mg

DIETARY EXCHANGES:
1 Starch/Bread, ½ Lean
Meat

SNACKING SURPRISE MUFFINS

Not just for breakfast anymore, muffins make great lunch box treats. Make each child's muffin different by filling it with their favorite flavor of fruit preserves!

1½ cups all-purpose flour
½ cup plus 1 tablespoon sugar, divided
1 cup fresh or frozen blueberries
2½ teaspoons baking powder
1¼ teaspoons ground cinnamon, divided
¼ teaspoon salt
1 egg, beaten
⅔ cup buttermilk
¼ cup margarine or butter, melted
3 tablespoons peach preserves

1 Preheat oven to 400°F. Line 12 medium-sized muffin cups with paper liners; set aside.

2 Combine flour, ½ cup sugar, blueberries, baking powder, 1 teaspoon cinnamon and salt in medium bowl. Combine egg, buttermilk and margarine in small bowl. Add to flour mixture; mix just until moistened.

3 Spoon about 1 tablespoon batter into each muffin cup. Drop a scant teaspoonful of preserves into center of batter in each cup; top with remaining batter.

4 Combine remaining 1 tablespoon sugar and ¼ teaspoon cinnamon in small bowl; sprinkle evenly over tops of batter.

5 Bake 18 to 20 minutes or until lightly browned. Remove muffins to wire rack to cool completely.
Makes 12 servings

Mini Red Hot Muffins: Omit preserves. Substitute mini muffin pan and miniature paper liners for regular-sized muffin pan and liners. Prepare batter as directed. Stir in 1 tablespoon red hot cinnamon candies. Spoon batter evenly into 24 prepared muffin cups, filling each cup ¾ full. Bake 14 to 16 minutes or until lightly browned.

Nutrients per Serving:

Calories	160
(25% of calories from fat)	
Total Fat	5 g
Saturated Fat	1 g
Cholesterol	18 mg
Sodium	178 mg
Carbohydrate	28 g
Dietary Fiber	1 g
Protein	3 g
Calcium	39 mg
Iron	1 mg
Vitamin A	57 RE
Vitamin C	2 mg

DIETARY EXCHANGES:
1½ Starch/Bread, ½ Fruit, ½ Fat

CINNAMON TRAIL MIX

More healthful than fat-laden chips, this spicy-sweet snack mix is sure to be a lunch box favorite for kids and adults alike.

Nutrients per Serving:

Calories	191
(18% of calories from fat)	
Total Fat	4 g
Saturated Fat	1 g
Cholesterol	0 mg
Sodium	260 mg
Carbohydrate	39 g
Dietary Fiber	1 g
Protein	3 g
Calcium	17 mg
Iron	3 mg
Vitamin A	38 RE
Vitamin C	10 mg

DIETARY EXCHANGES:
2½ Starch/Bread, ½ Fat

2 cups corn cereal squares
2 cups whole wheat cereal squares or whole wheat cereal squares with mini
    graham crackers
1½ cups fat free oyster crackers
½ cup broken sesame snack sticks
2 tablespoons margarine or butter, melted
1 teaspoon ground cinnamon
¼ teaspoon ground nutmeg
½ cup bite-sized fruit-flavored candy pieces

1 Preheat oven to 350°F. Spray 13×9-inch baking pan with nonstick cooking spray.

2 Place cereals, oyster crackers and sesame sticks in prepared pan; mix lightly.

3 Combine margarine, cinnamon and nutmeg in small bowl; mix well. Drizzle evenly over cereal mixture; toss to coat evenly.

4 Bake 12 to 14 minutes or until golden brown, stirring gently after 6 minutes. Cool completely. Stir in candies.

Makes 8 (¾-cup) servings

NO-BAKE GINGERSNAP BALLS

These gingersnap treats are a "snap" to prepare—so simple that the kids can even make them themselves!

20 gingersnap cookies (about 5 ounces)
3 tablespoons dark corn syrup
2 tablespoons creamy peanut butter
⅓ cup powdered sugar

1 Place cookies in large resealable plastic food storage bag; crush finely with rolling pin or meat mallet.

2 Combine corn syrup and peanut butter in medium bowl. Add crushed gingersnaps; mix well. (Mixture should hold together without being sticky. If mixture is too dry, stir in additional corn syrup 1 tablespoon at a time.)

3 Roll mixture into 24 (1-inch) balls; coat with powdered sugar.

Makes 8 servings

Nutrients per Serving:

Calories	138
(24% of calories from fat)	
Total Fat	4 g
Saturated Fat	1 g
Cholesterol	0 mg
Sodium	140 mg
Carbohydrate	25 g
Dietary Fiber	<1 g
Protein	2 g
Calcium	17 mg
Iron	2 mg
Vitamin A	0 RE
Vitamin C	0 mg

DIETARY EXCHANGES:
1½ Starch/Bread, ½ Fat

Cook's Tip

Some gingersnaps are crispier than others, so you may need to add an extra tablespoon, or two, of corn syrup to the crumb mixture in order to hold it together.

FRUIT AND OAT SQUARES

After tasting these scrumptious bars, you'll be amazed to learn that they're actually low in fat!

1 cup all-purpose flour
1 cup uncooked quick oats
¾ cup packed light brown sugar
½ teaspoon baking soda
¼ teaspoon salt
¼ teaspoon ground cinnamon
⅓ cup margarine or butter, melted
¾ cup apricot, cherry or other fruit flavored preserves

1 Preheat oven to 350°F. Spray 9-inch square baking pan with nonstick cooking spray; set aside.

2 Combine flour, oats, brown sugar, baking soda, salt and cinnamon in medium bowl; mix well. Add margarine; stir with fork until mixture is crumbly.

 Reserve ¾ cup crumb mixture for topping. Press remaining crumb mixture evenly onto bottom of prepared pan. Bake 5 to 7 minutes or until lightly browned.

4 Spread preserves onto crust; sprinkle with reserved crumb mixture.

5 Bake 20 to 25 minutes or until golden brown. Cool completely in pan on wire rack. Cut into 16 squares.

Makes 16 servings

Nutrients per Serving:

Calories	161
(23% of calories from fat)	
Total Fat	4 g
Saturated Fat	1 g
Cholesterol	0 mg
Sodium	123 mg
Carbohydrate	30 g
Dietary Fiber	<1 g
Protein	2 g
Calcium	18 mg
Iron	1 mg
Vitamin A	47 RE
Vitamin C	<1 mg

DIETARY EXCHANGES:
1½ Starch/Bread, ½ Fruit, ½ Fat

Cook's Tip
Store individually wrapped squares at room temperature up to 3 days or freeze up to 1 month.

BREAD PUDDING SNACKS

Comfort food for the lunch box! Wrap these individual snacks in pint-sized freezer bags and freeze up to 2 months. In the morning, pop one in your child's lunch. It will thaw by lunchtime and keep the other lunch box foods cold in the process.

1¼ cups 2% low fat milk
½ cup cholesterol free egg substitute
⅓ cup sugar
1 teaspoon vanilla
⅛ teaspoon ground nutmeg (optional)
⅛ teaspoon salt
4 cups (½-inch) cinnamon or cinnamon-raisin bread cubes (about 6 bread slices)
1 tablespoon margarine or butter, melted

1 Preheat oven to 350°F. Line 12 medium-sized muffin cups with paper liners.

2 Combine milk, egg substitute, sugar, vanilla, nutmeg and salt in medium bowl; mix well. Add bread; mix until well moistened. Let stand at room temperature 15 minutes.

3 Spoon bread mixture evenly into prepared cups; drizzle evenly with margarine.

4 Bake 30 to 35 minutes or until snacks are puffed and golden brown. Remove to wire rack to cool completely.

Makes 12 servings

Note: Snacks will puff up in the oven and fall slightly upon cooling.

Nutrients per Serving:

Calories	72
(22% of calories from fat)	
Total Fat	2 g
Saturated Fat	1 g
Cholesterol	2 mg
Sodium	93 mg
Carbohydrate	12 g
Dietary Fiber	0 g
Protein	2 g
Calcium	41 mg
Iron	<1 mg
Vitamin A	79 RE
Vitamin C	<1 mg

DIETARY EXCHANGES:
1 Starch/Bread

PLEASIN' PEANUTTY SNACK MIX

Both peanuts and peanut butter are great sources of niacin, a nutrient that helps to maintain healthy skin. Also, the insoluble fiber found in peanuts assists in keeping your digestive tract running smoothly.

4 cups whole wheat cereal squares *or* 2 cups whole wheat and 2 cups corn or rice cereal squares
2 cups small pretzel twists or goldfish-shaped pretzels
½ cup dry roasted peanuts
2 tablespoons creamy peanut butter
1 tablespoon honey
1 tablespoon apple juice or water
2 teaspoons vanilla
  Vegetable oil or butter flavored nonstick cooking spray
½ cup raisins, dried fruit bits or dried cherries (optional)

1 Preheat oven to 250°F.

2 Combine cereal, pretzels and peanuts in large bowl; set aside.

3 Combine peanut butter, honey and apple juice in 1-cup glass measure or small microwavable bowl. Microwave at HIGH 30 seconds or until hot. Stir in vanilla.

4 Drizzle peanut butter mixture evenly over cereal mixture; toss lightly to coat evenly. Place mixture in single layer in ungreased 15×10-inch jelly-roll pan; coat lightly with cooking spray.

5 Bake 8 minutes; stir. Continue baking 8 to 9 minutes or until golden brown. Remove from oven. Add raisins; mix lightly.

6 Spread mixture in single layer on large sheet of aluminum foil to cool.

Makes 10 (⅔-cup) servings

Nutrients per Serving:

Calories	174
(30% of calories from fat)	
Total Fat	6 g
Saturated Fat	1 g
Cholesterol	0 mg
Sodium	349 mg
Carbohydrate	26 g
Dietary Fiber	2 g
Protein	5 g
Calcium	14 mg
Iron	3 mg
Vitamin A	<1 RE
Vitamin C	10 mg

DIETARY EXCHANGES:
1½ Starch/Bread, 1 Fat

CINNAMON-RAISIN ROLL-UPS

A good source of vitamin A, carrots add vibrant color and great taste to this cinnamony-sweet snack.

Nutrients per Serving:

Calories	240
(32% of calories from fat)	
Total Fat	9 g
Saturated Fat	4 g
Cholesterol	25 mg
Sodium	127 mg
Carbohydrate	34 mg
Dietary Fiber	1 g
Protein	7 g
Calcium	31 mg
Iron	<1 mg
Vitamin A	448 RE
Vitamin C	2 mg

DIETARY EXCHANGES:
1½ Starch/Bread,
½ Lean Meat, ½ Fruit,
½ Vegetable, 1½ Fat

4 ounces Neufchâtel cheese, softened
½ cup shredded carrot
¼ cup golden or regular raisins
1 tablespoon honey
¼ teaspoon ground cinnamon
4 (7- to 8-inch) whole wheat or regular flour tortillas
8 thin apple wedges (optional)

1 Combine Neufchâtel cheese, carrot, raisins, honey and cinnamon in small bowl; mix well.

2 Spread tortillas evenly with Neufchâtel mixture, leaving ½-inch border around edge of each tortilla. Place 2 apple wedges down center of each tortilla; roll up. Wrap in plastic wrap. Refrigerate until ready to serve or pack in lunch box.

Makes 4 servings

Cook's Tip

For extra convenience, prepare roll-ups the night before. In the morning, pack a roll-up in a lunch box along with a frozen juice box. The juice box will thaw by lunchtime and keep the snack cold in the meantime!

School Party Snacks

SWEET HOLIDAYS PIZZA

Pizza is an American favorite. This dessert pizza contains all the flavors of an ice cream parlor sundae. You'll never believe it is low in fat!

Sweet Crumb Crust (page 52)
1½ pints (3 cups) vanilla or other desired flavor nonfat frozen yogurt, slightly softened
1½ pints (3 cups) chocolate or other desired flavor nonfat frozen yogurt, slightly softened
1 cup canned or fresh pineapple chunks
6 whole fresh strawberries, cut in half
1 cup thawed frozen peach slices *or* 1 medium peach, peeled and sliced
1 kiwi, peeled and sliced
12 pecan halves (optional)
¼ cup nonfat chocolate syrup, heated nonfat chocolate fudge sauce or favorite fruit flavored ice cream topping

1 Prepare Sweet Crumb Crust; freeze 15 minutes.

2 Spread vanilla yogurt onto crust to within ½ inch of edge; top with layer of chocolate yogurt. Cover with plastic wrap; freeze until firm, at least 6 hours or overnight.

3 Arrange fruits and nuts decoratively on top of pizza just before serving. Drizzle with chocolate syrup. Cut into wedges to serve. *Makes 16 servings*

(continued on page 52)

Nutrients per Serving:

Calories	302
(24% of calories from fat)	
Total Fat	8 g
Saturated Fat	1 g
Cholesterol	0 mg
Sodium	230 mg
Carbohydrate	53 g
Dietary Fiber	1 g
Protein	5 g
Calcium	15 mg
Iron	1 mg
Vitamin A	79 RE
Vitamin C	16 mg

DIETARY EXCHANGES:
3 Starch/Bread, ½ Fruit,
1 Fat

Sweet Holidays Pizza, continued

SWEET CRUMB CRUST

  2 cups graham cracker or vanilla wafer cookie crumbs
¼ cup sugar
¾ teaspoon ground cinnamon
  6 tablespoons margarine, melted

1 Line 12-inch pizza pan with aluminum foil; set aside.

2 Combine crumbs, sugar and cinnamon in medium bowl; stir in margarine. Place in prepared pizza pan; press mixture evenly onto bottom of pan.

Rocky Road Pizza: Omit vanilla frozen yogurt and fruits. Increase chocolate frozen yogurt to 1½ quarts (6 cups). Substitute 3 tablespoons chopped dry roasted peanuts for pecan halves. Prepare crust as directed. Spread yogurt onto crust as directed; cover and freeze until firm. Top with ¾ cup miniature marshmallows; sprinkle with peanuts. Drizzle with nonfat chocolate syrup.

Spumoni Pizza: Omit fruits. Reduce vanilla and chocolate frozen yogurts to 2 cups each. Add 2 cups slightly softened strawberry frozen nonfat yogurt. Substitute 3 tablespoons toasted slivered almonds for pecan halves. Prepare crust as directed. Spread yogurts onto crust as directed; cover and freeze until firm. Top with ½ cup each halved red and green maraschino cherries; sprinkle with almonds. Drizzle with nonfat chocolate syrup or strawberry ice cream topping.

Sweet Valentine Pizza: Omit pecan halves. Prepare crust as directed. Substitute 1½ quarts (6 cups) strawberry frozen nonfat yogurt for chocolate and vanilla frozen yogurts, and ½ to ¾ cup halved fresh strawberries for assorted fresh fruits. Spread yogurt onto crust as directed; cover and freeze until firm. Top with strawberries and pecans. Drizzle with nonfat chocolate syrup or strawberry ice cream topping.

TRICK OR TREAT ICE CREAM SANDWICHES

Fill cookies with orange sherbet for Halloween or your favorite flavor frozen yogurt for an anytime treat. The trick is on you when you discover how low in fat these are, too!

Nutrients per Serving:

Calories	184
(29% of calories from fat)	
Total Fat	6 g
Saturated Fat	1 g
Cholesterol	1 mg
Sodium	181 mg
Carbohydrate	31 g
Dietary Fiber	<1 g
Protein	2 g
Calcium	19 mg
Iron	1 mg
Vitamin A	50 RE
Vitamin C	1 mg

DIETARY EXCHANGES:
2 Starch/Bread, 1 Fat

½ cup margarine, softened
¾ cup granulated sugar
¾ cup packed light brown sugar
3 egg whites
1 teaspoon vanilla
2½ cups all-purpose flour
1½ teaspoons baking soda
1 teaspoon ground cinnamon
½ teaspoon salt
1 package (6 ounces) semisweet chocolate chips
1½ cups orange sherbet or any flavor nonfat frozen yogurt or ice cream, slightly softened

1 Preheat oven to 350°F. Spray baking sheets with nonstick cooking spray; set aside.

2 Beat margarine in large bowl until creamy. Add sugars; beat until fluffy. Blend in egg whites and vanilla. Combine flour, baking soda, cinnamon and salt in medium bowl. Add to margarine mixture; mix until well blended. Stir in chocolate chips.

3 Drop cookie dough by heaping teaspoonfuls onto prepared baking sheets, making 48 cookies. Bake until cookies are lightly browned, 10 to 12 minutes. Remove to wire racks to cool completely.

4 For each sandwich, place 1 tablespoon sherbet on flat side of 1 cookie; top with second cookie, flat side down. Press cookies together gently to even out sherbet layer. Repeat with remaining cookies and sherbet. Wrap tightly and store in freezer.

Makes 24 servings

(continued on page 54)

Trick or Treat Ice Cream Sandwiches, continued

Goblin Ice Cream Sandwiches: Prepare and freeze cookie sandwiches as directed. Just before serving, decorate 1 side of sandwich with Halloween candies or decorating gel to resemble goblin faces.

Colossal Cookie Sandwich: Substitute 2 lightly greased aluminum foil-lined 12-inch pizza pans for baking sheets. Substitute 1 quart (4 cups) frozen yogurt or ice cream for 1½ cups orange sherbet. Prepare cookie dough as directed; divide evenly in half. Spread each half evenly onto bottom of prepared pizza pan to within ½ inch of outer edge. Bake until cookies are lightly browned, 10 to 15 minutes. Cool cookies in pans just until cookies begin to firm; carefully slide off pans onto wire racks to cool completely. Spoon yogurt onto flat side of 1 cookie. Top with remaining cookie, flat side down. Freeze until yogurt is firm, about 6 hours. Cut into wedges to serve.

Sharing Cookies: Omit frozen yogurt. Bake cookies on pizza pans as directed for Colossal Cookie Sandwich; cool completely. Serve cookies whole on large platters, allowing each person to break off their own piece.

Cook's Tip

In a hurry? Soften the frozen sherbet, yogurt or ice cream in the microwave. Place measured amount in microwavable dish and microwave on MEDIUM-LOW (30%) 30 seconds or until slightly softened.

CHRISTMAS CONFETTI DIP

Vegetables galore make this festive dip a favorite with kids of all ages. You don't even need to tell them that it's good for them, too!

1 cup nonfat or reduced fat sour cream
4 teaspoons dry Ranch dressing mix
¼ cup finely chopped carrot
¼ cup finely chopped cucumber
¼ cup finely chopped red bell pepper
¼ cup finely chopped zucchini

1 Combine sour cream and dressing mix in medium bowl; mix well. Stir in chopped vegetables; cover. Refrigerate 2 to 3 hours for flavors to blend.

2 Transfer dip to medium serving bowl. Garnish with bell pepper cutouts, if desired. Serve with assorted fresh vegetable dippers. *Makes 8 (¼-cup) servings*

Dilly of a Dip: Substitute ½ cup finely chopped seeded cucumber for the 1 cup finely chopped vegetables listed above. Stir in 1 to 1½ teaspoons dill weed or dried basil leaves, crushed. *Makes about 1¾ cups*

Fresh Veggie Spread: Beat 1½ (8-ounce) packages softened nonfat or reduced fat cream cheese in medium bowl until creamy. Beat in enough nonfat or reduced fat sour cream to make desired consistency for spreading. Stir in 3 to 4 tablespoons *each* chopped red bell pepper, zucchini and carrot. Stir in 1 to 1½ teaspoons dill weed or dried oregano leaves, crushed. Spread onto assorted crackers or party rye bread slices. *Makes about 2 cups*

Quick Veggie Spread: Prepare Fresh Veggie Spread, substituting ¼ cup dry vegetable soup mix for the chopped fresh vegetables. *Makes about 1½ cups*

Nutrients per Serving:

(dip only)

Calories	31
(26% of calories from fat)	
Total Fat	1 g
Saturated Fat	<1 g
Cholesterol	1 mg
Sodium	37 mg
Carbohydrate	4 g
Dietary Fiber	<1 g
Protein	2 g
Calcium	41 mg
Iron	<1 mg
Vitamin A	259 RE
Vitamin C	17 mg

DIETARY EXCHANGES:
1 Vegetable

TACO POPCORN OLÉ

High in insoluble fiber and low in fat, popcorn is a great snack anytime. The butter flavored cooking spray in this savory south-of-the-border treat adds buttery flavor without the fat.

8 cups air-popped popcorn
  Butter flavored nonstick cooking spray
1 teaspoon chili powder
½ teaspoon salt
½ teaspoon garlic powder
⅛ teaspoon ground red pepper (optional)

1 Preheat oven to 350°F. Line 15×10-inch jelly-roll pan with aluminum foil.

2 Place popcorn in single layer in prepared pan. Coat lightly with cooking spray.

3 Combine chili powder, salt, garlic powder and red pepper in small bowl; sprinkle over popcorn. Mix lightly to coat evenly.

4 Bake 5 minutes or until hot, stirring gently after 3 minutes.

5 Spread mixture in single layer on large sheet of aluminum foil to cool.

Makes 8 (1-cup) servings

Nutrients per Serving:	
Calories	27
(2% of calories from fat)	
Total Fat	<1 g
Saturated Fat	0 g
Cholesterol	0 mg
Sodium	137 mg
Carbohydrate	5 g
Dietary Fiber	1 g
Protein	1 g
Calcium	3 mg
Iron	<1 mg
Vitamin A	11 RE
Vitamin C	<1 mg

DIETARY EXCHANGES:
Free Food

Cook's Tip
Store popcorn mixture in tightly covered container at room temperature up to 4 days.

FANTASY CINNAMON APPLEWICHES

A sprinkling of cinnamon-sugar adds just the right touch of spicy sweetness to this in-a-minute snack.

4 raisin bread slices
⅓ cup reduced fat cream cheese
¼ cup finely chopped unpeeled apple
1 teaspoon sugar
⅛ teaspoon ground cinnamon

1 Toast bread. Cut into desired shapes using large cookie cutters.

2 Combine cream cheese and apple in small bowl; spread onto toast.

3 Combine sugar and cinnamon in another small bowl; sprinkle evenly over cream cheese mixture.

Makes 4 servings

Nutrients per Serving:

Calories	119
(32% of calories from fat)	
Total Fat	5 g
Saturated Fat	2 g
Cholesterol	7 mg
Sodium	208 mg
Carbohydrate	17 g
Dietary Fiber	<1 g
Protein	4 g
Calcium	45 mg
Iron	1 mg
Vitamin A	83 RE
Vitamin C	<1 mg

DIETARY EXCHANGES:
1 Starch/Bread, 1 Fat

Cook's Tip

Get out the cookie cutters any time of the year for this fun treat. Or, create your own fun shapes—be sure to have an adult cut out your requested shape with a serrated knife for best results.

BAMBOOZLERS

These chocolatey treats have the chewy richness of brownies but contain only a small portion of the fat and calories.

Nutrients per Serving:

Calories	188
(31% of calories from fat)	
Total Fat	7 g
Saturated Fat	1 g
Cholesterol	18 mg
Sodium	79 mg
Carbohydrate	30 g
Dietary Fiber	<1 g
Protein	3 g
Calcium	28 mg
Iron	2 mg
Vitamin A	70 RE
Vitamin C	<1 mg

DIETARY EXCHANGES:
2 Starch/Bread, 1 Fat

1 cup all-purpose flour
¾ cup packed light brown sugar
¼ cup unsweetened cocoa powder
1 egg
2 egg whites
5 tablespoons margarine, melted
¼ cup skim milk
¼ cup honey
1 teaspoon vanilla
2 tablespoons semisweet chocolate chips
2 tablespoons coarsely chopped walnuts
    Powdered sugar (optional)

1 Preheat oven to 350°F. Grease and flour 8-inch square baking pan; set aside.

2 Combine flour, brown sugar and cocoa in medium bowl. Blend together egg, egg whites, margarine, milk, honey and vanilla in medium bowl. Add to flour mixture; mix well. Pour into prepared baking pan; sprinkle with chocolate chips and walnuts.

3 Bake brownies until they spring back when lightly touched in center, about 30 minutes. Cool completely in pan on wire rack. Sprinkle with powdered sugar just before serving.

Makes 12 servings

Peanutters: Substitute peanut butter chips for chocolate chips and peanuts for walnuts.

Butterscotch Babies: Substitute butterscotch chips for chocolate chips and pecans for walnuts.

Brownie Sundaes: Serve brownies on dessert plates. Top each brownie with a scoop of vanilla nonfat frozen yogurt and 2 tablespoons nonfat chocolate or caramel sauce.

Banana Bonanza: Serve brownies on dessert plates. Top each brownie with ¼ cup sliced banana and 2 tablespoons nonfat chocolate or caramel sauce.

ONE POTATO, TWO POTATO

Having a tough time getting your child to eat enough potatoes? After sampling these crispy low fat potato wedges, the kids will be begging for more!

Nonstick cooking spray
2 medium baking potatoes, cut lengthwise into 4 wedges
Salt
½ cup unseasoned dry bread crumbs
2 tablespoons grated Parmesan cheese (optional)
1½ teaspoons dried oregano leaves, dill weed, Italian herbs or paprika
Spicy brown or honey mustard, ketchup or reduced fat sour cream

1 Preheat oven to 425°F. Spray baking sheet with nonstick cooking spray; set aside.

2 Spray cut sides of potatoes generously with cooking spray; sprinkle lightly with salt.

3 Combine bread crumbs, Parmesan cheese and desired herb in shallow dish. Add potatoes; toss lightly until potatoes are generously coated with crumb mixture. Place on prepared baking sheet.

4 Bake potatoes until browned and tender, about 20 minutes. Serve warm as dippers with mustard.

Makes 4 servings

Potato Sweets: Omit Parmesan cheese, herbs and mustard. Substitute sweet potatoes for baking potatoes. Cut and spray potatoes as directed; coat generously with desired amount of cinnamon-sugar. Bake as directed. Serve warm as dippers with peach or pineapple preserves or honey mustard.

Nutrients per Serving:	
Calories	165
(5% of calories from fat)	
Total Fat	1 g
Saturated Fat	<1 g
Cholesterol	0 mg
Sodium	124 mg
Carbohydrate	36 g
Dietary Fiber	3 g
Protein	4 g
Calcium	50 mg
Iron	3 mg
Vitamin A	4 RE
Vitamin C	13 mg

DIETARY EXCHANGES:
2 Starch/Bread

BRONTOSAURUS BITES

A bounty of flavors and fun shapes makes this snack a great party take-home treat!

Nutrients per Serving:

Calories	194
(16% of calories from fat)	
Total Fat	4 g
Saturated Fat	<1 g
Cholesterol	0 mg
Sodium	81 mg
Carbohydrate	41 g
Dietary Fiber	2 g
Protein	2 g
Calcium	47 mg
Iron	1 mg
Vitamin A	16 RE
Vitamin C	25 mg

DIETARY EXCHANGES:
2 Starch/Bread, 1 Fruit,
1 Fat

4 cups air-popped popcorn
2 cups mini-dinosaur grahams
2 cups corn cereal squares
1½ cups dried pineapple wedges
1 package (6 ounces) dried fruit bits
    Butter flavored nonstick cooking spray
1 tablespoon plus 1½ teaspoons sugar
1½ teaspoons ground cinnamon
½ teaspoon ground nutmeg
1 cup yogurt-covered raisins

1 Preheat oven to 350°F. Combine popcorn, grahams, cereal, pineapple and fruit bits in large bowl; mix lightly. Transfer to 15×10-inch jelly-roll pan. Spray mixture generously with cooking spray.

2 Combine sugar, cinnamon and nutmeg in small bowl. Sprinkle ½ of the sugar mixture over popcorn mixture; toss lightly to coat. Spray mixture again with additional cooking spray. Add remaining sugar mixture; mix lightly.

3 Bake snack mix 10 minutes, stirring after 5 minutes. Cool completely in pan on wire rack. Add raisins; mix lightly.   *Makes 12 (¾-cup) servings*

Gorilla Grub: Substitute plain raisins for the yogurt-covered raisins and ¼ cup grated Parmesan cheese for the sugar, cinnamon and nutmeg.

Monkey Munchies: Substitute 2 cups low fat granola for 2 cups of the popcorn.

Rabbit Rations: Substitute chocolate mini-rabbit grahams for the dinosaur grahams and dried banana chips for the dried pineapple.

Cook's Tip
For individual party take-home treats, wrap snack mix in festive colored paper napkins.

SOFT PRETZELS

Now you can create the warm chewy goodness of soft pretzels in your own kitchen! You and your child will delight in transforming this tantalizing dough into a fun array of festive holiday shapes.

Nutrients per Serving:

Calories	214
(23% of calories from fat)	
Total Fat	6 g
Saturated Fat	1 g
Cholesterol	20 mg
Sodium	315 mg
Carbohydrate	33 g
Dietary Fiber	<1 g
Protein	8 g
Calcium	62 mg
Iron	2 mg
Vitamin A	81 RE
Vitamin C	<1 mg

DIETARY EXCHANGES:
2 Starch/Bread, ½ Lean
Meat, 1 Fat

1 package (16 ounces) hot roll mix, plus ingredients to prepare mix
1 egg white
2 teaspoons water
2 tablespoons *each* assorted coatings: grated Parmesan cheese, sesame seeds, poppy seeds, dried oregano leaves

1 Prepare hot roll mix according to package directions.

2 Preheat oven to 375°F. Spray baking sheets with nonstick cooking spray; set aside.

3 Divide dough equally into 16 pieces; roll each piece with hands to form a rope, 7 to 10 inches long. Place on prepared cookie sheets; form into desired shape (hearts, wreaths, pretzels, snails, loops, etc.).

4 Beat together egg white and water in small bowl until foamy. Brush onto dough shapes; sprinkle each shape with 1½ teaspoons of one of the coatings.

5 Bake until golden brown, about 15 minutes. Serve warm or at room temperature.

Makes 8 servings

Fruit Twists: Omit coatings. Prepare dough and roll into ropes as directed. Place ropes on lightly floured surface. Roll out, or pat, each rope into rectangle, ¼ inch thick; brush each rectangle with about 1 teaspoon spreadable fruit or preserves. Fold each rectangle lengthwise in half; twist into desired shape. Bake as directed.

Cheese Twists: Omit coatings. Prepare dough and roll into rectangles as directed in Fruit Twists. Sprinkle each rectangle with about 1 tablespoon shredded Cheddar or other cheese. Fold dough rectangles, shape and bake as directed for Fruit Twists.

ROCK 'N' ROLLERS

For a change of pace, serve these satisfying tortilla roll-ups at your child's next party. High in both calcium and vitamin C, they're as good for you as they are tasty.

4 (6- to 7-inch) flour tortillas
4 ounces Neufchâtel cheese, softened
⅓ cup peach preserves
1 cup (4 ounces) shredded nonfat Cheddar cheese
½ cup packed washed fresh spinach leaves
3 ounces thinly sliced regular or smoked turkey breast

1 Spread each tortilla evenly with 1 ounce Neufchâtel cheese; cover with thin layer of preserves. Sprinkle with Cheddar cheese.

2 Arrange spinach leaves and turkey over Cheddar cheese. Roll up tortillas; trim ends. Cover and refrigerate until ready to serve.

3 Cut "rollers" crosswise in half or diagonally into 1-inch pieces.

Makes 8 servings

Sassy Salsa Rollers: Substitute salsa for peach preserves and shredded iceberg lettuce for spinach leaves.

Ham 'n' Apple Rollers: Omit peach preserves and spinach leaves. Substitute lean ham slices for turkey. Spread tortillas with Neufchâtel cheese as directed; sprinkle with Cheddar cheese. Top each tortilla with about 2 tablespoons finely chopped apple and 2 ham slices; roll up. Continue as directed.

Wedgies: Prepare Rock 'n' Rollers or any variation as directed, but do not roll up. Top with a second tortilla; cut into wedges.

Nutrients per Serving:	
Calories	339
(26% of calories from fat)	
Total Fat	10 g
Saturated Fat	5 g
Cholesterol	48 mg
Sodium	505 mg
Carbohydrate	40 g
Dietary Fiber	1 g
Protein	22 g
Calcium	332 mg
Iron	2 mg
Vitamin A	169 RE
Vitamin C	2 mg

DIETARY EXCHANGES:
2½ Starch/Bread, 2 Lean Meat, 1 Fat

Cook's Tip
To celebrate the holidays, tint the Neufchâtel cheese with food color to fit the season—pink for Valentine's Day, green for St. Patrick's Day or red and green for Christmas. Or, for a special holiday touch, dip ends of rollers into minced parsley and garnish with a piece of red pimento.

AFTER SCHOOL MUNCHIES

SNACKIN' BANANA SPLIT

Reward your youngster for those good grades with this luscious low fat snack!

1 ripe small banana, peeled
1 small scoop vanilla nonfat or low fat frozen yogurt (about 3 tablespoons)
1 small scoop strawberry nonfat or low fat frozen yogurt (about 3 tablespoons)
⅓ cup sliced fresh strawberries or blueberries
2 tablespoons no-sugar-added strawberry fruit spread
1 teaspoon hot water
2 tablespoons low fat granola cereal
1 maraschino cherry (optional)

1 Split banana in half lengthwise. Place in shallow bowl; top with frozen yogurt and strawberries.

2 Combine fruit spread and water in small bowl; mix well. Spoon over yogurt; sprinkle with granola. Top with cherry, if desired.   *Makes 1 serving*

Nutrients per Serving:

Calories	359
(6% of calories from fat)	
Total Fat	3 g
Saturated Fat	<1 g
Cholesterol	0 mg
Sodium	88 mg
Carbohydrate	87 g
Dietary Fiber	3 g
Protein	4 g
Calcium	22 mg
Iron	1 mg
Vitamin A	11 RE
Vitamin C	38 mg

DIETARY EXCHANGES:
2 Starch/Bread, 3½ Fruit,
½ Fat

PERFECT PITA PIZZAS

Have each child design their own funny face on their individual pizza!

2 whole wheat or white pita bread rounds
½ cup spaghetti or pizza sauce
¾ cup (3 ounces) shredded part-skim mozzarella cheese
1 small zucchini, sliced ¼ inch thick
½ small carrot, peeled and sliced
2 cherry tomatoes, halved
¼ small green bell pepper, sliced

1 Preheat oven to 375°F. Cover baking sheet with foil; set aside.

2 Using small scissors, carefully split each pita bread round around edge; separate to form 2 rounds.

3 Place rounds, rough sides up, on prepared baking sheet. Bake 5 minutes.

4 Spread 2 tablespoons spaghetti sauce onto each round; sprinkle with cheese. Decorate with vegetables to create faces. Bake 10 to 12 minutes or until cheese melts.

Makes 4 servings

Pepperoni Pita Pizzas: Prepare pita rounds, partially bake and top with spaghetti sauce and cheese as directed. Place 2 small pepperoni slices on each pizza for eyes. Decorate with cut-up fresh vegetables for rest of face. Continue to bake as directed.

Nutrients per Serving:

Calories	183
(26% of calories from fat)	
Total Fat	6 g
Saturated Fat	3 g
Cholesterol	17 mg
Sodium	431 mg
Carbohydrate	26 g
Dietary Fiber	3 g
Protein	9 g
Calcium	159 mg
Iron	1 mg
Vitamin A	364 RE
Vitamin C	21 mg

DIETARY EXCHANGES:
1 Starch/Bread, 1 Lean Meat, 1½ Vegetable, ½ Fat

MICROWAVE CHOCOLATE PUDDING

Nothing hits the spot better on a cold, rainy day than this creamy, rich, homemade pudding. Made with 2% milk and cocoa powder, this low fat version of the classic dessert is the perfect comfort food.

⅓ cup sugar
¼ cup unsweetened cocoa powder
2 tablespoons cornstarch
1½ cups 2% low fat milk
1 teaspoon vanilla
⅛ teaspoon ground cinnamon (optional)
    Assorted small candies (optional)

1 Combine sugar, cocoa powder and cornstarch in medium microwavable bowl or 1-quart glass measure. Gradually add milk, stirring with wire wisk until well blended.

2 Microwave at HIGH 2 minutes; stir. Microwave at MEDIUM-HIGH (70%) 3½ to 4½ minutes or until thickened, stirring every 1½ minutes.

3 Stir in vanilla and cinnamon. Let stand at least 5 minutes before serving, stirring occasionally to prevent skin from forming. Serve warm or chilled. Garnish with candies just before serving, if desired.

Makes 4 servings

Nutrients per Serving:

Calories	139
(14% of calories from fat)	
Total Fat	2 g
Saturated Fat	1 g
Cholesterol	7 mg
Sodium	50 mg
Carbohydrate	28 g
Dietary Fiber	<1 g
Protein	4 g
Calcium	120 mg
Iron	2 mg
Vitamin A	56 RE
Vitamin C	1 mg

DIETARY EXCHANGES:
1 Starch/Bread, ½ Milk, ½ Fat

BROCCOLI-CHEESE QUESADILLAS

These delicious quesadillas can be made ahead, wrapped individually and stored in the refrigerator or freezer

1 cup (4 ounces) shredded nonfat Cheddar cheese
½ cup finely chopped fresh broccoli
2 tablespoons picante sauce or salsa
4 (6- to 7-inch) corn or flour tortillas
1 teaspoon margarine, divided

1 Combine cheese, broccoli and picante sauce in small bowl; mix well.

2 Spoon ¼ of the cheese mixture onto 1 side of each tortilla; fold tortilla over filling.

3 Melt ½ teaspoon margarine in 10-inch nonstick skillet over medium heat. Add 2 quesadillas; cook about 2 minutes on each side or until tortillas are golden brown and cheese is melted. Repeat with remaining margarine and quesadillas. Cool completely.

Makes 4 servings

Nutrients per Serving:

Calories	109
(13% of calories from fat)	
Total Fat	2 g
Saturated Fat	<1 g
Cholesterol	5 mg
Sodium	313 mg
Carbohydrate	14 g
Dietary Fiber	1 g
Protein	11 g
Calcium	304 mg
Iron	1 mg
Vitamin A	99 RE
Vitamin C	13 mg

DIETARY EXCHANGES:
1 Starch/Bread, 1 Lean Meat

Cook's Tip
Refrigerate individually wrapped quesadillas up to
2 days or freeze up to 3 weeks.

BANANA FREEZER POPS

Make these tasty pops after school one day to enjoy the next. While fun to eat, each one is loaded with potassium and vitamin C.

2 ripe medium bananas
1 can (6 ounces) frozen orange juice concentrate, thawed (¾ cup)
¼ cup water
1 tablespoon honey
1 teaspoon vanilla
8 (3-ounce) paper or plastic cups
8 wooden sticks

1 Peel bananas; break into chunks. Place in food processor or blender container.

2 Add orange juice concentrate, water, honey and vanilla; process until smooth.

3 Pour banana mixture evenly into cups. Cover top of each cup with small piece of aluminum foil. Insert wooden stick through center of foil into banana mixture.

4 Place cups on tray; freeze until firm, about 3 hours. To serve, remove foil; tear off paper cups (or slide out of plastic cups). *Makes 8 servings*

Peppy Purple Pops: Omit honey and vanilla. Substitute grape juice concentrate for orange juice concentrate.

Frozen Banana Shakes: Increase water to 1½ cups. Prepare fruit mixture as directed. Add 4 ice cubes; process on high speed until mixture is thick and creamy. *Makes 3 servings*

Nutrients per Serving:

Calories	70
(2% of calories from fat)	
Total Fat	<1 g
Saturated Fat	<1 g
Cholesterol	0 mg
Sodium	1 mg
Carbohydrate	17 g
Dietary Fiber	1 g
Protein	1 g
Calcium	9 mg
Iron	<1 g
Vitamin A	8 RE
Vitamin C	35 mg

DIETARY EXCHANGES:
1 Fruit

TORTELLINI TEASERS

Colorful kabobs teamed with this zesty sauce make a great kid-pleasin' snack that's high in vitamin A.

Zesty Tomato Sauce (recipe follows)
½ (9-ounce) package refrigerated cheese tortellini
1 large red or green bell pepper, cut into 1-inch pieces
2 medium carrots, peeled and sliced ½ inch thick
1 medium zucchini, sliced ½ inch thick
12 medium fresh mushrooms
12 cherry tomatoes

1 Prepare Zesty Tomato Sauce; keep warm until ready to use.

2 Cook tortellini according to package directions; drain.

3 Alternate 1 tortellini and 2 to 3 vegetable pieces on long frilled wooden picks or wooden skewers. Serve as dippers with tomato sauce.   *Makes 6 servings*

ZESTY TOMATO SAUCE

1 can (15 ounces) tomato purée
2 tablespoons finely chopped onion
2 tablespoons chopped fresh parsley
1 teaspoon dried oregano leaves, crushed
¼ teaspoon dried thyme leaves, crushed
¼ teaspoon salt
⅛ teaspoon black pepper

1 Combine tomato purée, onion, parsley, oregano, thyme, salt and black pepper in small saucepan. Heat thoroughly, stirring occasionally. Garnish with carrot curl, if desired.

Ravioli Teasers: Substitute ravioli for tortellini.

Perky Pestos: Substitute ⅓ cup purchased pesto sauce for Zesty Tomato Sauce. Heat sauce and drizzle over kabobs.

Nutrients per Serving	
(2 kabobs)	
Calories	136
(13% of calories from fat)	
Total Fat	2 g
Saturated Fat	1 g
Cholesterol	9 mg
Sodium	448 mg
Carbohydrate	26 g
Dietary Fiber	4 g
Protein	6 g
Calcium	34 mg
Iron	2 mg
Vitamin A	901 RE
Vitamin C	71 mg

DIETARY EXCHANGES:
½ Starch/Bread,
3 Vegetable, ½ Fat

SUPER NACHOS

What child doesn't like nachos? This low fat version of everyone's favorite Mexican appetizer is sure to become an everyday request.

12 large baked low fat tortilla chips (about 1½ ounces)
½ cup (2 ounces) shredded reduced fat Cheddar cheese
¼ cup fat free refried beans
2 tablespoons chunky salsa

1 Arrange chips in single layer on large microwavable plate. Sprinkle cheese evenly over chips.

2 Spoon teaspoonfuls of beans over chips; top with ½ teaspoonfuls of salsa.

3 Microwave at MEDIUM (50%) 1½ minutes; rotate dish. Microwave 1 to 1½ minutes or until cheese is melted.

Makes 2 servings

Conventional Directions: Substitute aluminum foil-covered baking sheet for microwavable plate. Assemble nachos as directed on prepared baking sheet. Bake at 350°F, 10 to 12 minutes or until cheese is melted.

Nutrients per Serving:	
Calories	176
(26% of calories from fat)	
Total Fat	5 g
Saturated Fat	2 g
Cholesterol	16 mg
Sodium	683 mg
Carbohydrate	23 g
Dietary Fiber	2 g
Protein	10 g
Calcium	210 mg
Iron	1 mg
Vitamin A	81 RE
Vitamin C	5 mg

DIETARY EXCHANGES:
1½ Starch/Bread, 1 Lean Meat, ½ Fat

Cook's Tip

For a single serving of nachos, arrange 6 large tortilla chips on microwavable plate; top with ¼ cup cheese, 2 tablespoons beans and 1 tablespoon salsa. Microwave at MEDIUM (50%) 1 minute; rotate dish. Continue to microwave 30 seconds to 1 minute or until cheese is melted.

INSIDE-OUT TURKEY SANDWICHES

You'll find the "bread" on the inside of this tasty snack!

2 tablespoons nonfat cream cheese
2 tablespoons pasteurized process cheese spread
2 teaspoons chopped green onion tops
1 teaspoon prepared mustard
12 thin round slices fat free turkey breast or smoked turkey breast
4 large pretzel logs or unsalted bread sticks

1 Combine cream cheese, process cheese spread, green onion and mustard in small bowl; mix well.

2 Arrange 3 turkey slices on large sheet of plastic wrap, overlapping slices in center. Spread ¼ of cream cheese mixture evenly onto turkey slices, covering slices completely. Place 1 pretzel at bottom edge of turkey slices; roll up turkey around pretzel. (Be sure to keep all 3 turkey slices together as you roll them around pretzel.)

3 Repeat with remaining ingredients.

Makes 4 servings

Nutrients per Serving:

Calories	112
(18% of calories from fat)	
Total Fat	2 g
Saturated Fat	1 g
Cholesterol	6 mg
Sodium	567 mg
Carbohydrate	12 g
Dietary Fiber	<1 g
Protein	10 g
Calcium	54 mg
Iron	<1 mg
Vitamin A	39 RE
Vitamin C	<1 mg

DIETARY EXCHANGES:
½ Starch/Bread, 1 Lean Meat

FROZEN CHOCOLATE-COVERED BANANAS

A delightful twist on frozen ice pops, these luscious, chocolate-dipped bananas are high in potassium, a mineral which helps maintain the proper functioning of the heart and kidneys.

2 ripe medium bananas
4 wooden sticks
½ cup low fat granola cereal without raisins
⅓ cup hot fudge sauce, at room temperature

1 Cover baking sheet or 15×10-inch jelly-roll pan with waxed paper; set aside.

2 Peel bananas; cut each in half crosswise. Insert wooden stick into center of cut end of each banana about 1½ inches into banana half. Place on prepared baking sheet; freeze until firm, at least 2 hours.

3 Place granola in large plastic food storage bag; crush slightly using rolling pin or meat mallet. Transfer granola to shallow plate. Place fudge sauce in a shallow dish.

4 Working with 1 banana at a time, place frozen banana in fudge sauce; turn banana and spread fudge sauce evenly onto banana with small rubber scraper. Immediately place banana on plate with granola; turn to coat lightly. Return to baking sheet in freezer. Repeat with remaining bananas.

5 Freeze until fudge sauce is very firm, at least 2 hours. Place on small plates; let stand 5 minutes before serving.

Makes 4 servings

Nutrients per Serving:

Calories	163
(21% of calories from fat)	
Total Fat	4 g
Saturated Fat	2 g
Cholesterol	0 mg
Sodium	25 mg
Carbohydrate	32 g
Dietary Fiber	1 g
Protein	3 g
Calcium	36 mg
Iron	1 mg
Vitamin A	17 RE
Vitamin C	5 mg

DIETARY EXCHANGES:
1 Starch/Bread, 1 Fruit,
½ Fat

CHEESY BARBECUED BEAN DIP

This tasty dip, which heats in less than 2 minutes, is a great way for children to enjoy those vitamin-filled vegetables.

½ cup canned vegetarian baked beans
3 tablespoons pasteurized process cheese spread
2 tablespoons regular or hickory smoke flavored barbecue sauce
2 large carrots, peeled and diagonally sliced
1 medium red or green bell pepper, cut into chunks

1 Place beans in small microwavable bowl; mash slightly with fork. Stir in process cheese spread and barbecue sauce. Cover with plastic wrap; vent.

2 Microwave at HIGH 1 minute; stir. Microwave 30 seconds or until hot. Garnish with green onion and bell pepper cutouts, if desired. Serve with carrot and bell pepper dippers.

Makes 4 servings

Nutrients per Serving:

Calories	93
(25% of calories from fat)	
Total Fat	3 g
Saturated Fat	1 g
Cholesterol	10 mg
Sodium	355 mg
Carbohydrate	15 g
Dietary Fiber	4 g
Protein	4 g
Calcium	70 mg
Iron	1 mg
Vitamin A	1409 RE
Vitamin C	131 mg

DIETARY EXCHANGES:
1 Starch/Bread, ½ Fat

Personalized Nutrition Reference for Different Calorie Levels*

Age Group	1–3 years about 30 lbs.	4–6 years about 45 lbs.	7–10 years about 60 lbs.
Daily Calorie Level	1300	1800	2000
Total Fat**	no limit	60 g	67 g
% of Calories from Fat**	no limit	30%	30%
Saturated Fat**	no limit	18 g	20 g
Carbohydrate (% of calorie levels)	40–50%	55–60%	55–60%
Protein	16 g	24 g	28 g
Dietary Fiber***	6–8 g	9–11 g	10–15 g
Cholesterol**	no limit	300 mg	300 mg
Calcium	800 mg	800 mg	800 mg
Iron	10 mg	10 mg	10 mg
Vitamin A	400 RE	500 RE	700 RE
Vitamin C	40 mg	45 mg	45 mg

* Numbers may be rounded and calorie levels will vary between the sexes.

** Due to the fact that both fat and cholesterol are paramount to the development of the brain, limiting fat for children between the ages of 1 and 3 is not recommended, even if a child is overweight.

*** Total grams of recommended dietary fiber is based on the child's age plus 5.

Note: For specific advice concerning calorie levels, please consult a registered dietitian, qualified health professional or pediatrician.

VOLUME MEASUREMENTS (dry)

⅛ teaspoon = 0.5 mL
¼ teaspoon = 1 mL
½ teaspoon = 2 mL
¾ teaspoon = 4 mL
1 teaspoon = 5 mL
1 tablespoon = 15 mL
2 tablespoons = 30 mL
¼ cup = 60 mL
⅓ cup = 75 mL
½ cup = 125 mL
⅔ cup = 150 mL
¾ cup = 175 mL
1 cup = 250 mL
2 cups = 1 pint = 500 mL
3 cups = 750 mL
4 cups = 1 quart = 1 L

VOLUME MEASUREMENTS (fluid)

1 fluid ounce (2 tablespoons) = 30 mL
4 fluid ounces (½ cup) = 125 mL
8 fluid ounces (1 cup) = 250 mL
12 fluid ounces (1½ cups) = 375 mL
16 fluid ounces (2 cups) = 500 mL

WEIGHTS (mass)

½ ounce = 15 g
1 ounce = 30 g
3 ounces = 90 g
4 ounces = 120 g
8 ounces = 225 g
10 ounces = 285 g
12 ounces = 360 g
16 ounces = 1 pound = 450 g

DIMENSIONS

1/16 inch = 2 mm
⅛ inch = 3 mm
¼ inch = 6 mm
½ inch = 1.5 cm
¾ inch = 2 cm
1 inch = 2.5 cm

OVEN TEMPERATURES

250°F = 120°C
275°F = 140°C
300°F = 150°C
325°F = 160°C
350°F = 180°C
375°F = 190°C
400°F = 200°C
425°F = 220°C
450°F = 230°C

BAKING PAN SIZES

Utensil	Size in Inches/Quarts	Metric Volume	Size in Centimeters
Baking or	8×8×2	2 L	20×20×5
Cake Pan	9×9×2	2.5 L	22×22×5
(square or	12×8×2	3 L	30×20×5
rectangular)	13×9×2	3.5 L	33×23×5
Loaf Pan	8×4×3	1.5 L	20×10×7
	9×5×3	2 L	23×13×7
Round Layer	8×1½	1.2 L	20×4
Cake Pan	9×1½	1.5 L	23×4
Pie Plate	8×1¼	750 mL	20×3
	9×1¼	1 L	23×3
Baking Dish	1 quart	1 L	—
or Casserole	1½ quart	1.5 L	—
	2 quart	2 L	—